Bruno's

A Speech/Language Book on Positional Words

Steph Winkeler

Let's Connect! Visit simplicityhappens.com and subscribe to receive adorable, language and cognitive development activities for children ages 2-6!

Bruno's Ball

Independently Published by S.L. Winkeler

For permission requests contact: simplicityhappens@gmail.com

Published in the United States of America

ISBN: 978-1-079-54411-4

For my Little Bear. May you always find what you're looking for on every adventure!

Note from the Author

This story was created for my toddler, an adventurous little boy with tons of energy. He is the inspiration for all that I do. I wanted to help support his understanding of common vocabulary and positional concepts within an interactive literacy format. Our family cherishes the time we have reading books together each day. Thus, I'd like to share a piece of our reading time with you through the story of Bruno and his favorite red ball.

Bruno's Ball is meant to create a positive and encouraging dialogue between parent/caregiver and child in the following ways:

- *Bruno's Ball* is designed for children ages 18 months to 6 years old and includes an interactive story dialogue, and story vocabulary and positional concepts (with supplemental tracking sheets included) for use as your child develops and grows their knowledge of vocabulary words and positional concepts.

- When the story asks, "Where is Bruno's ball?," give your child time to look for and locate the red ball. Once your child identifies the ball's location (e.g., pointing/labeling, responding), continue with the story and respond by adding more language dialogue for your child to hear (e.g., "Yes!" There's the red ball." "It's in the window."). The textual framework is there to help guide you through this interactive dialogue with your child.

I sincerely hope *Bruno's Ball* invites adventure, dialogue and excitement during your family reading time. Wishing you memorable reading moments with your little ones.

Sincerely,

Steph Winkeler, *Speech-Language Therapist*

P.S. Don't forget to look for the secret password to unlock more *Bruno's Ball* activities!

Table of Contents

Bruno is a happy puppy. He's playing outside.
He loves chasing his favorite red ball.
Where is Bruno's ball?
It's in the window.

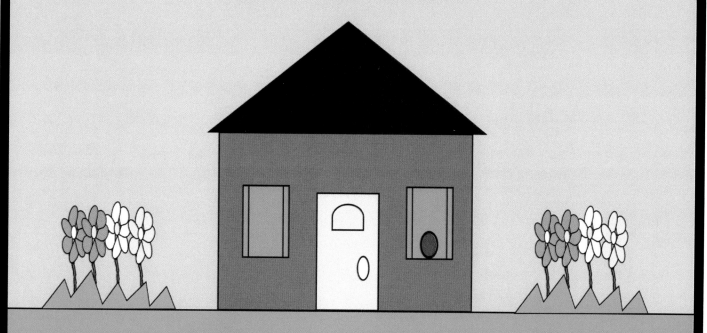

1

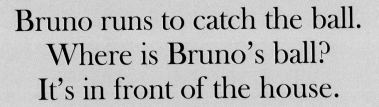

Bruno runs to catch the ball.
Where is Bruno's ball?
It's in front of the house.

Uh oh! Bruno lost his ball.
Let's help Bruno find the ball.
Where is Bruno's ball?
It's behind the flowers!

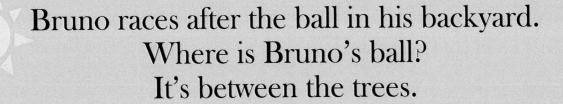

Bruno races after the ball in his backyard.
Where is Bruno's ball?
It's between the trees.

4

Bruno chases his red ball at the park.
Where is Bruno's ball?
It's next to the bird.

Bruno sprints toward the playground.
Where is Bruno's ball?
It's under the monkey bars.

Bruno chases his ball into the open field.
Where is Bruno's ball?
It's on top of the rock.

Bruno dashes to the pond.
Where is Bruno's ball?
It's in the pond.

Bruno darts to the other side of the pond.
Where is Bruno's ball?
It's behind the pond.

Bruno races around the pond.
Where is Bruno's ball?
It's next to the rock.

Bruno scurries into the playground.
Where is Bruno's ball?
It's on top of the bear tunnel.

Bruno chases his ball out of the park.
Where is Bruno's ball?
It's between the flowers.

Bruno follows the ball into his backyard.
Where is Bruno's ball?
It's under the tree.

Bruno hurries to the front yard.
Where is Bruno's ball?
It's in front of the door.

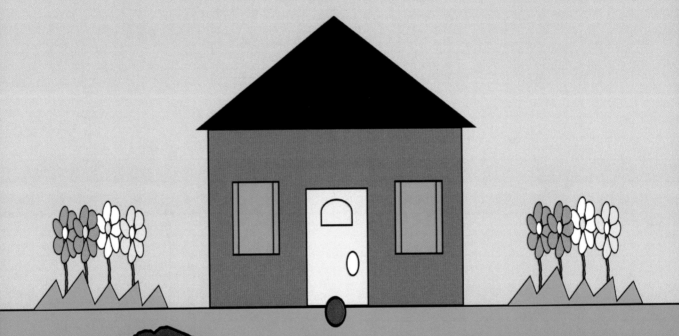

Bruno has had so much fun chasing after his ball.
He's finally home and ready for a nap.
Where is Bruno's ball?
Bruno has the ball, and he's not going to let it go!

Notes

Thanks for helping me
find my favorite red ball!

It's so fun learning
positional words with you!

Bruno's Ball: Vocabulary Concepts

sun

house

bird

tree

turtle

ball

Bruno

flowers

rock

Vocabulary Concepts: Receptive Tracking Sheet

Ask your child, "Where is the...(bird)? Place a check mark in the box next to the vocabulary words that your child <u>receptively</u> identifies (e.g., pointing) within the story or on the picture vocabulary page (p. 19).

Where is the...?

bird	☐
ball	☐
swing	☐

Where is the...?

house	☐
rock	☐
park	☐

Where is the...?

tree	☐
window	☐

Where is...?

Bruno	☐

<u>Notes</u>

_____

_____

_____

_____

18

Picture Vocabulary

bird

house

Bruno

ball

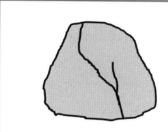
rock

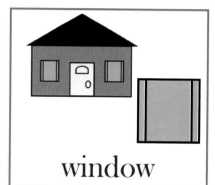
window

swing

park

tree

19

Vocabulary Concepts: Expressive Tracking Sheet

Point to a picture and ask your child, "What is this?" Place a check mark in the box next to the vocabulary words that your child <u>expressively</u> states within the story or on the picture vocabulary page (p. 21).

What is this?

a bird ☐

a ball ☐

a swing ☐

What is this?

a house ☐

a rock ☐

a park ☐

What is this...?

a tree ☐

a window ☐

Who is this?

Bruno ☐

<u>Notes</u>

_____

_____

_____

_____

20

Picture Vocabulary

bird

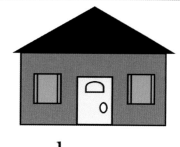
house

Bruno

ball

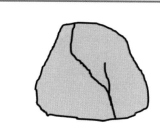
rock

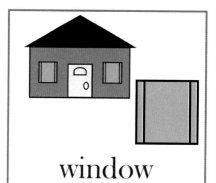
window

swing

park

tree

Vocabulary Concepts: Receptive Tracking Sheet

Ask your child, "Where is the...(sun)? Place a check mark in the box next to the vocabulary words that your child <u>receptively</u> identifies (e.g., pointing) within the story or on the picture vocabulary page (p. 23).

Where is the...?

sun	☐

Where is the...?

playground	☐

Where is the...?

door	☐

slide	☐

turtle	☐

Where are the...?

flowers	☐

bear tunnel	☐

pond	☐

monkey bars	☐

<u>Notes</u>

_____

_____

_____

_____

22

Picture Vocabulary

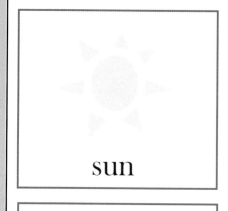

sun

playground

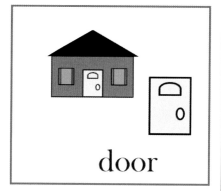

door

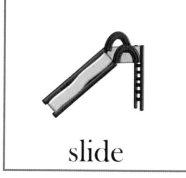

slide

turtle

flowers

bear tunnel

pond

monkey bars

Vocabulary Concepts: Expressive Tracking Sheet

Point to a picture and ask your child, "What is this?" Place a check mark in the box next to the vocabulary words that your child <u>expressively</u> states within the story or on the picture vocabulary page (p. 25).

What is this?

a sun	☐

a slide	☐

a bear tunnel	☐

What is this?

a playground	☐

a turtle	☐

a pond	☐

What is this?

a door	☐

What are these?

flowers	☐

monkey bars	☐

<u>Notes</u>

_____

_____

_____

_____

24

Picture Vocabulary

sun

playground

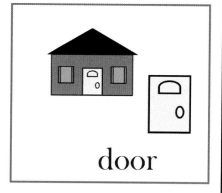
door

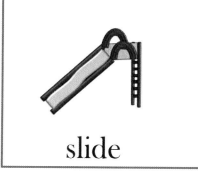
slide

turtle

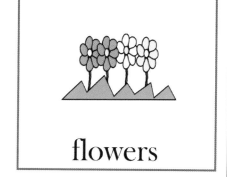
flowers

bear tunnel

pond

monkey bars

Notes

Bruno's Ball: Positional Concepts

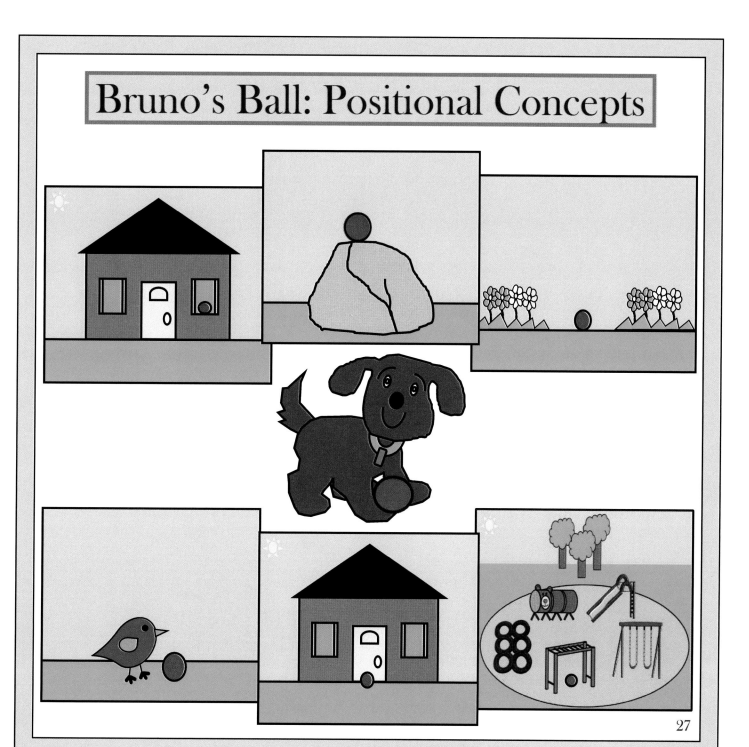

Positional Concepts: Tracking Sheet

Place a check mark in the box next to the positional concepts that your child identifies, receptively, on p. 29 (e.g., see "Receptive" below). Once your child identifies positional concepts receptively (e.g., pointing), ask them to tell you where the ball is within each picture (e.g., see "Expressive" below).

<u>Receptive</u> ☐
Show me where Bruno's ball is *on top* of the rock? (b)

<u>Expressive</u> ☐
Tell me where Bruno's ball is in this picture? (b)

<u>Receptive</u> ☐
Show me where Bruno's ball is *in front* of the rock? (a)

<u>Expressive</u> ☐
Tell me where Bruno's ball is in this picture? (a)

<u>Receptive</u> ☐
Show me where Bruno's ball is *next to* the rock? (d)

<u>Expressive</u> ☐
Tell me where Bruno's ball is in this picture? (d)

<u>Receptive</u> ☐
Show me where Bruno's ball is *behind* the rock? (c)

<u>Expressive</u> ☐
Tell me where Bruno's ball is in this picture? (c)

Positional Concepts

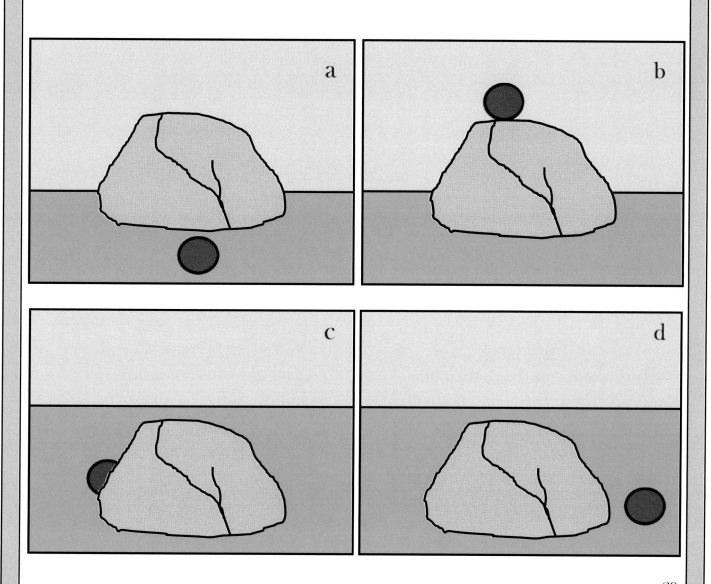

Positional Concepts: Tracking Sheet

Place a check mark in the box next to the positional concepts that your child identifies, receptively, on p. 31 (e.g., see "Receptive" below). Once your child identifies positional concepts receptively (e.g., pointing), ask them to tell you where the ball is within each picture (e.g., see "Expressive" below).

<u>Receptive</u> ☐	<u>Expressive</u> ☐
Show me where Bruno's ball is *on top* of the monkey bars? (b)	Tell me where Bruno's ball is in this picture? (b)

<u>Receptive</u> ☐	<u>Expressive</u> ☐
Show me where Bruno's ball is *next to* the monkey bars? (c)	Tell me where Bruno's ball is in this picture? (c)

<u>Receptive</u> ☐	<u>Expressive</u> ☐
Show me where Bruno's ball is *behind* the monkey bars? (d)	Tell me where Bruno's ball is in this picture? (d)

<u>Receptive</u> ☐	<u>Expressive</u> ☐
Show me where Bruno's ball is *under* the monkey bars? (a)	Tell me where Bruno's ball is in this picture? (a)

Positional Concepts

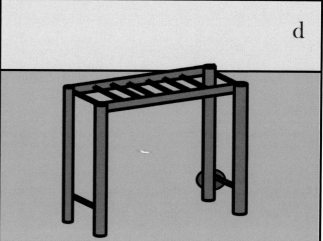

31

Positional Concepts: Tracking Sheet

Place a check mark in the box next to the positional concepts that your child identifies, receptively, on p. 33 (e.g., see "Receptive" below). Once your child identifies positional concepts receptively (e.g., pointing), ask them to tell you where the ball is within each picture (e.g., see "Expressive" below).

<u>Receptive</u> ☐ Show me where Bruno's ball is *behind* the flowers? (a)	<u>Expressive</u> ☐ Tell me where Bruno's ball is in this picture? (a)
<u>Receptive</u> ☐ Show me where Bruno's ball is *on top* of the flowers? (d)	<u>Expressive</u> ☐ Tell me where Bruno's ball is in this picture? (d)
<u>Receptive</u> ☐ Show me where Bruno's ball is *between* the flowers? (b)	<u>Expressive</u> ☐ Tell me where Bruno's ball is in this picture? (b)
<u>Receptive</u> ☐ Show me where Bruno's ball is *in front* of the flowers? (c)	<u>Expressive</u> ☐ Tell me where Bruno's ball is in this picture? (c)

Positional Concepts

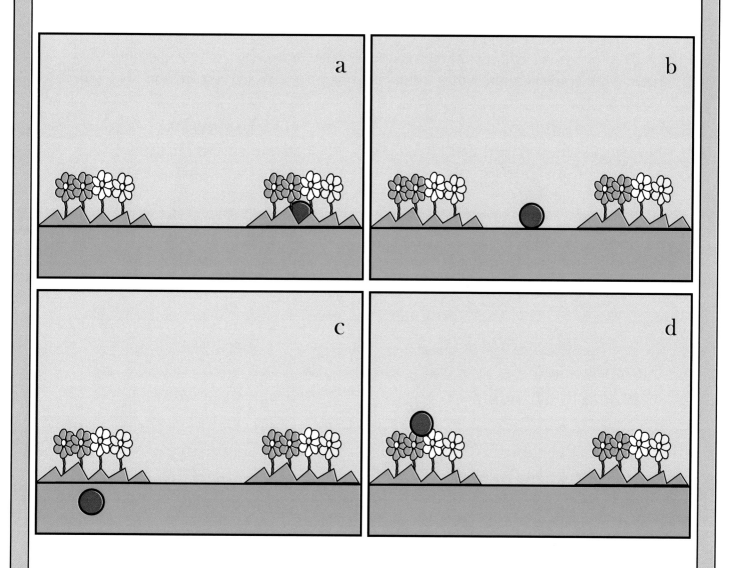

Positional Concepts: Tracking Sheet

Place a check mark in the box next to the positional concepts that your child identifies, receptively, on p. 35 (e.g., "Show me where Bruno's ball is on top?"). Note: Add words in parenthesis for extra support (e.g., "Show me where Bruno's ball is on top of the rock?"). Once your child identifies positional concepts receptively (e.g., pointing), ask them to tell you where the ball is within each picture (e.g., see "Expressive" below).

Receptive ☐	Expressive ☐
Show me where Bruno's ball is *on top* (of the rock)? (b)	Tell me where Bruno's ball is in this picture? (b)

Receptive ☐	Expressive ☐
Show me where Bruno's ball is *between* (the trees)? (d)	Tell me where Bruno's ball is in this picture? (d)

Receptive ☐	Expressive ☐
Show me where Bruno's ball is *behind* (the pond)? (c)	Tell me where Bruno's ball is in this picture? (c)

Receptive ☐	Expressive ☐
Show me where Bruno's ball is *in* (the window)? (a)	Tell me where Bruno's ball is in this picture? (a)

Positional Concepts

a

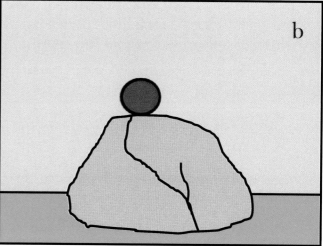

b

c

d

Positional Concepts: Tracking Sheet

Place a check mark in the box next to the positional concepts that your child identifies, receptively, on p. 37 (e.g., "Show me where Bruno's ball is in front?"). Note: Add words in parenthesis for extra support (e.g., "Show me where Bruno's ball is in front of the house?"). Once your child identifies positional concepts receptively (e.g., pointing), ask them to tell you where the ball is within each picture (e.g., see "Expressive" below).

Receptive ☐	Expressive ☐
Show me where Bruno's ball is *between* (the flowers)? (a)	Tell me where Bruno's ball is in this picture? (a)

Receptive ☐	Expressive ☐
Show me where Bruno's ball is *in front* (of the house)? (c)	Tell me where Bruno's ball is in this picture? (c)

Receptive ☐	Expressive ☐
Show me where Bruno's ball is *next to* (the bird)? (b)	Tell me where Bruno's ball is in this picture? (b)

Receptive ☐	Expressive ☐
Show me where Bruno's ball is *under* (the slide)? (d)	Tell me where Bruno's ball is in this picture? (d)

Positional Concepts

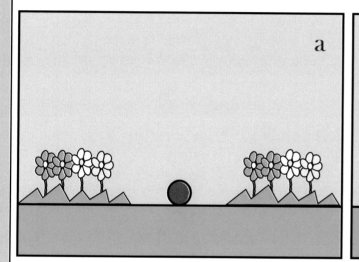

Positional Concepts: Tracking Sheet

Place a check mark in the box next to the positional concepts that your child identifies on p. 39 (e.g., "Show me where Bruno's ball is behind?"). Note: Add words in parenthesis for extra support (e.g., "Show me where Bruno's ball is behind the flowers?"). Once your child identifies positional concepts receptively (e.g., pointing), ask them to tell you where the ball is within each picture (e.g., see "Expressive" below).

Receptive ☐	Expressive ☐
Show me where Bruno's ball is *behind* (the flowers)? (c)	Tell me where Bruno's ball is in this picture? (c)

Receptive ☐	Expressive ☐
Show me where Bruno's ball is *in* (the pond)? (b)	Tell me where Bruno's ball is in this picture? (b)

Receptive ☐	Expressive ☐
Show me where Bruno's ball is *under* (the monkey bars)? (a)	Tell me where Bruno's ball is in this picture? (a)

Receptive ☐	Expressive ☐
Show me where Bruno's ball is *next to* (the rock)? (d)	Tell me where Bruno's ball is in this picture? (d)

Positional Concepts

a

b

c

d

Positional Concepts: Tracking Sheet

Place a check mark in the box next to the positional concepts that your child identifies on p. 41 (e.g., "Show me where Bruno's ball is next to?"). Note: Add words in parenthesis for extra support (e.g., "Show me where Bruno's ball is next to the swing?"). Once your child identifies positional concepts receptively (e.g., pointing), ask them to tell you where the ball is within each picture (e.g., see "Expressive" below).

<u>Receptive</u> ☐ Show me where Bruno's ball is *in front* (of the door)? (c)	<u>Expressive</u> ☐ Tell me where Bruno's ball is in this picture? (c)
<u>Receptive</u> ☐ Show me where Bruno's ball is *under* (the tree)? (b)	<u>Expressive</u> ☐ Tell me where Bruno's ball is in this picture? (b)
<u>Receptive</u> ☐ Show me where Bruno's ball is *next to* (the swing)? (d)	<u>Expressive</u> ☐ Tell me where Bruno's ball is in this picture? (d)
<u>Receptive</u> ☐ Show me where Bruno's ball is *on top* (of the bear tunnel)? (a)	<u>Expressive</u> ☐ Tell me where Bruno's ball is in this picture? (a)

40

Positional Concepts

a

b

c

d

Dear Reader,

   Thank you for sharing Bruno's Ball with your little ones! I would love to hear from you! If you have a moment, please share a review on Amazon about your reading experience with Bruno's Ball! Your insights are greatly appreciated and beneficial for future speech/language story books!

Sincerely,
Steph Winkeler

Check Out the following Speech/Language Books by Steph Winkeler
Use the QR Codes (next to cover photo) or search for the books on Amazon!

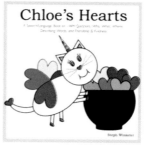 

Your LITTLE ones will love being BIG helpers as they guide Teddy, a determined gingerbread cookie, on finding his way home. Go on a BIG & LITTLE learning adventure together when you read *Teddy's Travels* with your little ones. This book is perfect for the fall and winter seasons with lovable characters and delicious candy along the way.

Join Chloe, a compassionate unicorn cat, on her travels as she learns how the simple act of sharing creates the magic of kindness & kinship. Support your child's understanding of Who, What, & Where Questions, Color Knowledge, and Describing Words when you share the magical story of Chloe's Hearts with your little ones!

Follow Hattie, Ziggy, and Pixie, three hard-working honeybees, as they set out together to search for flowers and collect nectar for making delicious golden honey! Create teachable moments with your little ones when you give the directions to,

"Point to the first bee."
"Point to the bee in the middle."
"Point to the last bee."

Help Addy, an adventurous little girl, discover the magical crown, map, and cape to harness her superpowers and find the buried treasure on the island of *Cool Cove* while learning story vocabulary words with initial /k/ & /g/ sounds. Your little ones can use the power of problem-solving by listening for clues and answering questions as they find their own superpowers during this playful treasure hunt adventure.

Made in the USA
Middletown, DE
14 January 2023

22135054R00029